Tall Birds Stalking

Also by Michael Van Walleghen

The Wichita Poems, 1975

More Trouble with the Obvious, 1981

Blue Tango, 1989

Tall
Birds
Stalking

Michael Van Walleghen

University of Pittsburgh Press
Pittsburgh • London

The publication of this book is supported by a grant from the Pennsylvania Council on the Arts.

Published by the University of Pittsburgh Press, Pittsburgh, Pa. 15260

Copyright © 1994, Michael Van Walleghen

All rights reserved

Manufactured in the United States of America

Printed on acid-free paper

A CIP catalogue record for this book is available from the British Library.

Eurospan, London

Library of Congress Cataloging-in-Publication Data

Van Walleghen, Michael, 1938–
    Tall birds stalking / Michael Van Walleghen.
        p.   cm. —(Pitt Poetry Series)
    ISBN 0-8229-3794-8 (cl.).—ISBN 0-8229-5529-6 (pbk.)
    I. Title.   II. Series.
    PS3572.A545T35   1994   94-11759
    811'.54—dc20   CIP

A CIP catalogue record for this book is available from the British Library.

Eurospan, London

The author and publisher wish to express their grateful acknowledgment to the following publications in which some of these poems first appeared: *The Cimarron Review* ("Rush Hour," "The Unbearable Part"); *Crazyhorse* ("Album Epilepticus," "The Hunk," "Uncle Jerry"); *Passages North* ("Late," "Long Division"); *Prairie Schooner* ("The Brave Adventure," "Catch Him!," "Missed Connections"); and *The Southern Review* ("Adios Zarathustra," "Crawlspace," "Tall Birds Stalking").

"The Awards Banquet" and "In the Chariot Drawn by Dragons" first appeared in *The Hudson Review*.

Paperback cover painting and section divider artwork by James G. Davis, courtesy of Riva Yares Gallery, Scottsdale, Ariz.

Author photo by Harry Zanoff, Creative Images

Book design by Frank Lehner

In memory of my father
and my brother, Jim

Contents

Tall Birds Stalking

The Light

On a cloudy day
on a day the clouds
the lake the late
small sun seem stopped
and the gray birds
dive like stones
or drift high
petrified and small
against the light
against that symbol, metaphor
and old analogy
to which the heart
perpetually aspires,
on such a day,
even Icarus
might have turned
and walked into the marsh,
noticed by tall birds stalking
and the glittering fishes
that, cloudlike,
move away.

from THE WICHITA POEMS, *1975*

1

Adios Zarathustra

They were watching it
for a niece who watched
their dog last summer:

a geriatric cockatoo
named Zarathustra

who could ride a scooter
talk dirty, and sometimes
properly coaxed, squawk

a few strangled bars
of the "Star Spangled Banner."

It also loved mirrors
bright dangly earrings
and being out of its cage—

like a privileged trustee
they thought, some harmless

old lifer who had learned
long since, that Alcatraz
was Alcatraz—inescapable

and the only home he had.
Where could he want to go?

But when he saw his chance
when they let the dog out once
it was adios Zarathustra—

gone: a small white hanky
waving from the lilacs . . .

They posted notices of course
which likewise disappeared—
Buddhistic little prayers

fluttering in the laundromat
gas station, grocery store . . .

until finally it was winter
and dark by five o'clock . . .
Nothing could save him now.

Which eschatological fact
their niece, a young woman

in her twenties, engaged
and just back from Europe
could accept with a shrug.

Why get all worked up? An old
mean-tempered bird like that . . .

While they, on the other hand,
wrestling his cage back down
from its vain, crabapple bower

were depressed by his mirrors
and earrings for months . . .

And they had other feelings too—
curious, heartbreaking dreams
they were ashamed, at first

to confess. Love dreams
involving different people

from as far back as college—
everyone they had ever liked
or gone to bed with it seemed—

some of them dead by now
some of them still beautiful

lost out there in the snow
in the land of the free
the home of the brave.

The Beaufort Sea

A morning of dense fog
and sudden trucks—

their tiny brake lights
growing dimly bright

at the very last instant
a scant ten feet ahead . . .

each light reminding him
of someone anxious, cold

and probably exhausted—
dogwatch lookouts maybe

somewhere in the Beaufort Sea
dragging on their cigarettes.

The barometer falling again
the ice pack closing in . . .

And then, at last, a sign—
huge, unmistakable even here

at the end of the world: *Chicago
and O'Hare,* it says, *Keep Left.*

Chicago? Is it possible?
What happened to St. Louis?

Get the navigator up here
on the double! But already

it's clear: unless he finds
the fabled Northwest Passage

then circumnavigates the globe
he's stuck out here forever—

forever on this Beaufort Sea
of catastrophic, cold divorce

where now he's out of smokes
and almost out of whisky . . .

dim icebergs, like giant trucks
drifting close on either side.

The Unbearable Part

Steps, railings, gutters
everything was rotten
even the roof . . .

He couldn't go on like that

living alone on food stamps
the place filling up with newspapers
garbage, God knows what . . .

But the worst part
the really unbearable part
was the dog. Half-starved

trembling, surrounded
by bones, sticks, sinister
odd scraps of fur

by stove parts, car junk
and the frozen rubble
of his own dumb shit

he never barked
but over and over again
all night, all winter

we'd hear his chain run out
and then this little grunt
that always left us worried

as if we might be listening
to someone in the next room
strangling in their sleep.

This went on till March.
Then his sister Betty
drove up from St. Louis

with a big dump truck
and some young people
from her Bible group.

What a job! They scraped
hauled and hammered around
all weekend. They painted

and trimmed the hedges.
They even planted flowers.
But the dog, I noticed

looked flatly unconvinced—
the sharklike button
of his bad right eye

fixed on something else—
something in that vatic dark
beyond all fixing . . .

But what could Betty know?
Or anyone for that matter?
She just moved herself in

and the next weekend
after it got cold again
all of them were dead—

Mr. Green, Betty, the dog . . .

Asphyxiation the fireman said.
Dead birds in the chimney.
Leaves, loose mortar . . .

But it's the dog finally
I can't stop thinking about—
I seem to hear him now

even in my sleep: first
the rattle of his chain
and then that other sound

I can't quite place . . .
But waking up of course
I understand everything:

a few leaves rattling
between the houses maybe—
my wife tossing in her sleep

then the furnace coming on.

Missed Connections

—January 1, 1990

It's three o'clock
New Year's morning

and snowing a little
outside the frazzled

bright empty dreamscape
of the blue Dayton airport . . .

It seems we've missed
our last connection—

no limousine, no minibus
a flagpole somewhere

clanking in the wind . . .
the whole surly crowd

of calamitous flight 1066
sans luggage, milling around

on the sidewalk, looking
for someone to talk to

the moron in charge here
a taxi for Christsake

to take us to our hotel.
Then the lights go out

and someone's dazed, dead
on his feet six year old

decides to lie down now
and sleep on the cement

like a sudden flashback
to some forgotten war . . .

No one can leave the city.
Anyone out after curfew

excepting military personnel
and selectees for transport

will be shot on sight—
children will be shot

and somewhere, a flagpole
might rattle in the wind

or a train might whistle
it's light coming toward us

like the light at the end
of our dark millennium.

2

Tall Birds Stalking

1. *The Moon Over the AMOCO Sign*

That long first day
after fifteen hours

of Illinois, Kentucky
Tennessee and Georgia

any vacancy would do—
a barn, a chicken coop . . .

but we drove on forever
until we came to heaven

our daughter's dream
come true, a real motel

complete with water slide
and *Jaws* on HBO. Three

or four drinks later
relaxed, half-paralyzed

on our little balcony
I watch the full moon

the merest apparition
a mirage of some kind

float improbably up
from behind a Pizza Hut

then turn completely real
just above the AMOCO sign

on the bypass heading south
where my father was dying . . .

Gangrene again. Another leg.
This time above the knee.

Inside our flickering room
my daughter's movie screams

and screams. Tomorrow
when we get to the Gulf

she'll be afraid to swim—
imagining the bloody water

dismembered arms and legs
the endless, true abyss

where an ordinary moon
was shining, even now.

2. What's My Name?

Strange machines
have landed on the roof
outside my father's window . . .

and so my mother sighs
pulls down the shade

and starts asking questions:

What's my name?
she wants to know.
Who am I? Whereupon

confused, frightened
by all this urgency

flower feathered birds
that live on morphine
flutter in the curtains.

There! my father points.
There! as if the room
were really full of names

flying frantically about
looking for a place to land . . .

but they're only birds
and quite as nameless

as the air-conditioner
taking off again, rising
out there on the roof

like Charon's helicopter
or some terrible angel
from the Apocalypse . . .

Meanwhile, his black
altogether anonymous foot
is resting on its pillow.

Another face almost—
wide-awake, monstrous

to which, all afternoon
our helpless eyes advert

as if we'd heard it cough
clear its throat a little

and even try to speak.

3. *Tall Birds Stalking*

Dawn. On the horizon
a single mushroom cloud

has grown up overnight
from the jade green Gulf
like a real mushroom . . .

but because it is not
the end of the world

but only Tuesday, Monday
or maybe Wednesday . . . the day
anyway, after the delivery

of his father's small ashes
from the Cremation Society

a grown man and his mother
are walking on the beach
discussing life insurance.

Arguing in the air above them
the usual flock of innocuous birds . . .

And then, up ahead, a fisherman
casting from the stone jetty
strikes a fish, a giant snook

or shark or even barracuda
that takes out all his line.

The grown man and his mother
the retired couple collecting
sharks' teeth—all of them

stop dead in their tracks.
This is interesting. This

reminds them of something
dangerous: a fall perhaps
down icy steps, a stroke . . .

and then that final, headlong
acceleration of the spirit

out among the galaxies—
the cold, starry ocean
where it feels at home . . .

A tall, blue gray heron
another rock until now

stabs a piece of lost bait
from a crevice. The fisherman
sits down tired on his bucket

and the grown man, everyone,
knows just how he feels

having been there before
in that hieroglyphic of grief
with tall birds stalking.

Album Epilepticus

—for Jim

1. *Double Exposure*

One Christmas, broke, broke
and unemployable, my brother

presented us with a small
framed picture of himself:

a baby so disdainfully held
in my loose, ten-year-old arms

so obviously loathed just then
for all his cross–eyed yearning

it seemed to my wife and me
but more emphatically to him

who suffered most the late
and helpless rage between us

some almost perfect paradigm
a kind of comic, sibling X-ray

of all we could have wished
were otherwise. Otherwise

that Christmas went as fated:
he'd refuse to take his pills

drink until he couldn't walk
then have a grand mal seizure . . .

then yet another in the car
beside me, moaning in the dark

his head banging on the window
all the way to the hospital

and details I'd since forgotten:
that little tree the nurses had

the sad, incongruous mistletoe
and then my baby brother there

his baby fingers blue, my father
crying in the waiting room

while I walked up and down
with mother in the hall.

2. Bad Light

His lights had been on
day and night for days

and he hadn't paid the rent.
His landlady was worried . . .
No one answered over there.

His new, Salvation Army chair
his broken couch and bed . . .

When the phone rang, these
and certain other fleabag comforts
came rushing sharply into focus

and stayed there, portentous
as the furniture of dreams . . .

I could see his filthy toilet
his grayish yellow curtains—
all the shipwrecked clutter

of his moldy kitchen, his icebox
the month of dishes in the sink.

But where was he? What weekend
trip or idyll? Perhaps the judge
who refused him Social Security

had invited him out for a sail
or maybe the doctor who whined

because he didn't have Blue-Cross
and thus refused to treat him
had taken him skiing at Vail.

I could see how it might happen.
I could see him running off

with a movie star, winning
the lottery, living in France—
I could imagine anything . . .

except, of course, his lights
were on, the television too.

So when we finally knocked
then broke his stupid door
that empty light was blinding—

so bright, I could barely see
through the bedroom bead chains

his phone and bedside radio
or in the black, reflecting window
the shotgun lying on the floor.

3. *The Cremains of Morpheus Hecuba*

It was the first snow
of the season—little pellets
of hard ice really, that stung
and made us turn our faces . . .

But once inside the funeral home
it was much too hot. Something
was wrong with the thermostat

and the room where we waited
hummed with bad connections.

There were forms we had to sign
certain things about my brother
that were hard to remember . . .

Wasn't there a bank account?
Insurance? Any property at all?

Beside me, on a bamboo table
a large, blue butterfly floated
in a cube of clear plastic. "That"
said the director, "is a rare
specimen. A *Morpheus Hecuba*."

Then, after one last signature
he handed over my brother's ashes.

"CREMAINS" the hand–typed label read.

And in the same ink–filled letters
it irked me to notice, as *MORPHEUS
HECUBA: rare, shade-loving butterfly
of the Amazon basin*—on a little
card that had fallen to the floor.

Some months later however, in March
when I thought to look this dryad up
by way of finding another poem maybe
I found there was no such thing.

Only the rather common *Morpho
Hecuba, Hecuba*—and some others
like it, from the same family.

My brother's ashes rested still
in limbo then, at the bottom
of my filing cabinet—heavier
than I could bear to lift . . .

But soon enough, it was almost
Easter. What were we thinking?
It was time to have it over.

So we drove down to my mother's
place, in Florida. We had decided
to bury the ashes there, beside
my father's, under the avocado
in her garden. We did it quickly

and long after dark, Good Friday.
Overhead, an airplane blinked on
and off among some billion stars
all common to that tropical sky—

a blizzard that stung just then
and made us turn our faces . . .

as Hecuba herself may have turned
from Hector's burning, remembering
now his infant, sweet blue eyes
and how she sang them closed.

Rest in peace, we said. Sleep
sleep we whispered . . .

3

In the Chariot Drawn by Dragons

Such a chariot has Helios, my father's father,
Given me to defend me from my enemies.
—Euripides, Medea

Fascinating the way our dreams
accommodate the muddled here

and now—the phone we answer
in our sleep for instance
before it startles us awake

or just this morning, the cat
killing something in the yard—

a baby rabbit it turns out
squealing that one high note
only nightmares comprehend . . .

the one where real children
lie dismembered in their beds—

as, indeed, I heard it spoken
on the evening news . . . Medea
of course, was never mentioned

although I understood at once
the way we often do in dreams

that it was she again—disguised
in this last, horrific incarnation
to look like almost anyone . . .

a forgotten second cousin say
whose husband studied neutron

stars, black holes . . . matters
so quantum mechanically intense
so distant, it would take her

nearly fifteen billion years
of living practically abandoned

in married student housing
with two frenetic, infant sons
and no help at all from anyone

before she understood at last
that everything was hopeless—

that nothing, not even light
not the merest glimmer of it
could ever escape such gravity—

a force so crushing in the end
she could barely lift the knife

and wake us up again, heart
pounding, to some poor rabbit
screaming as the sun comes up

or Medea in her bloody bathrobe
and the chariot drawn by dragons.

With Tyler at the Temple of Pain and Remembering

He bumps his way late
into room 123, his chair

festooned with slogans
wisecracks—a plastering

of cautionary stickers
reminding us to KEEP OUT

FUCK OFF, or otherwise
emphatically BEWARE

the PIT BULL WITH AIDS
asleep invisibly there

gorged on bloody dreams:
broken bones, dismemberment.

Last week's chainsaw horror
and the phallic white worm

we find guarding the temple
of PAIN and REMEMBERING

at the end of this week's poem
which we are about to discuss—

our worksheets rustling now
like the murmurous leaves

of that selfsame dismal wood
where even Dante lost his way . . .

the very wood of Tyler's poem
wherein the leopard dwells

the lion and slathering wolf . . .
as well as certain other things—

like cave bears for instance.
Scorpions. The man-eating apes

who fuck in his closet . . .
not to mention of course

that curious Cyclopean worm
who finally takes off screaming

all coiling and uncoiling
when the trees catch fire

then dies twisting in the sea
below the cliff-close temple

where we have just arrived
completely out of breath—

too tired now to speak . . .
stunned by the heavy shields

glittering, chased in silver
and the many fine tripods

both bronze and of iron
that lie around him there

where everything he owns
is on display, and holy.

Uncle Jerry

After poor Aunt Vonnie
lapsed into her coma

and became a "vegetable"
weighing no more we guessed
than fifty fetal pounds

Uncle Jerry, bless his heart
spared absolutely nothing

bribing everyone who asked
until he had her placed at last
in that nameless, private home

for whacked-out millionaires
so as to bathe her everyday

then feed her through a tube
in her half-pint stomach
another fifteen years. Who

ever heard of such devotion!
Nor was that the least of it.

A religious man, Uncle Jerry
was sure they'd meet again
in heaven—or later maybe

at the noisy Resurrection.
In any case, he'd be ready.

He owned the leafy gravesite
next to hers. Casket, headstone
everything was all arranged—

except . . . he had these doubts.
What if she wasn't down there?

They do that you know. Sell you
an expensive bill of goods
then pull the old switcharoo

and sell it all over again. Or
suppose they just made a mistake?

Anyway, he couldn't stand it.
The thought of being buried
next to some complete stranger—

another man perhaps, who knows?
was making him sick. And so

five years after the funeral
he had her dug up again
just to make sure. Everyone

even Uncle Jerry, was amazed
at how much of her was left.

But what a relief! Eternity
safe and cozy once again . . .
And as long as he was at it

why not build a mausoleum?
That way he could have a key

and visit any time he liked—
all those warm spring nights
his flashlight woke the birds

and the white wisteria foamed
in moonlight near the door.

4

Fishing with Dracula
on the Dark Vermilion

Thigh-deep before dawn
in the swift, cold water

the far bank just visible
the dim trees twittering

he hears, behind him now
that curious, watery panic

he's heard before in dreams—
a sound like leaves at first

rattling in an empty doorway
then leaves turned sudden fish

in a shudder of piranha memory . . .
But when he turns to look

he finds, instead, an owl
struggling there to rise—

huge, the size of Dracula
it seems to him, so fierce

are his eyes, so audibly close
the concussive slap of his wings

as he lifts a corpse-sized fish
to his nest beneath the bridge.

How else to understand it then
but as some sign or metaphor

wherein the owl must be himself
and years of childhood nightmare

become the river where he fishes—
this rock-strewn, dawn Vermilion

sliding by, like life itself
so fast it's hard to stand in.

And literally vermilion too—
blood-red as the sun comes up

over the red, autumnal trees . . .
From the air, how would it look?

Mile on mile of reflected leaves
spilling from some blown aorta . . .

although an owl might see fish
down there—occasional, like poems

without language yet, mere inklings . . .
bringing to mind that other hunter

the one in camouflage fatigues
and the silver, one-way glasses

who watched him from the bridge
just yesterday, through the scope

of a semiautomatic deer rifle
for one full minute, thinking

it over, how the blood might look
before he smiled and waved hello.

Something He Forgets

Yes, but what do you think about
all that time?
                    —Anon.

1

Before the dream–disguised
bedside alarm quits ringing
he answers the telephone . . .

But it's for someone else—
a brother who's left already

or hasn't returned just yet
from some fishing trip or other . . .
And then he's disconnected, staring

at 5:00 A.M. blinking on the radio
which has fallen to the floor.

Beyond the gray windows, pigeons—
their fluttery moans and grunts
giving birth to light somehow.

2

In the driveway, loading the boat
what is it he's forgotten? Battery
tackle box, landing net . . . And yet

every time he checks his list again
something crucial seems to disappear—

a thing so humble, so pedestrian
he could look right at it probably
and never see it. His lost thermos

43

for instance, a gift from his brother
just weeks before he shot himself . . .

But here it is at last, wedged tight
under the bow seat, as if hidden there
like a shoe with the foot still in it.

3

He has to be careful backing up now
because a thick fog has obliterated
the public boat ramp. *Watch it*

he tells himself. *Easy.* But he can't
quite see the lake he's aiming for . . .

or the boat either. If he's not careful
he could go bubbling down with the car
into fifty feet of water . . . Meanwhile

what a curious sensation, this jerking
back and back through the systolic

blood red mist of the brake lights—
like being born perhaps, or how a soul
might feel, embarking on the boat of Ra.

4

An hour later and it's clear again—
safe to fish in the bleached forest
of flooded trees, the still waters

scummed with algae and croaking now
like the very engine of his thought:

he could have done something, called
stopped by, invited him to dinner . . .
He could have been better, friendlier

the brother his brother wanted him
to be. They could have gone fishing

and sat here together, not speaking—
listening to frogs and a woodpecker
hammering out the obvious in code.

5

Last night, in his dream, his brother
drowns again—then, he's alive somehow
and walking around in an old boathouse

talking to himself—the boats all
restless, bumping and making noise . . .

But then the phone rings and things
get suddenly quiet, like right now
out here on the lake. It's the wind

he thinks, a creaking in the trees
to which the whole swamp listens

like someone listening on a telephone
that's rung all day for no one there
beside the clock and broken radio.

Crawlspace

In coastal Florida
where my mother lives

the old are everywhere
but some feel younger

by the minute. *Terrific!*
Never better! my mother's

diabetic neighbor shouts
from her tipsy lawn tractor.

I'm like a kid down here!
Everyday vicissitude however

that water-dance of local light
partakes of something different

something ancient and Egyptian—
like red tides, for instance

or those nightmare catfish
that walk around like lizards.

That's why, playing pinochle
our conversation turns to snakes—

a recent python in particular
all twenty-one feet of it

police and zoo officials
have to extricate by hand

from the feculent crawlspace
beneath the yacht-club restaurant.

There's even a picture of it
in the paper: *Long Lost Pet*

Found at Last . . . but nervous
and with an appetite for dogs.

Then it's time to have a drink
and consider citrus canker

or mothlike flakes of snow
that kill the oranges overnight.

We're all like kids down here . . .
our fathers, our lovely mothers

having all gone off somewhere
leaving us alone and listening

to something awful moving
in the leaves beneath the house.

The Hunk

—Florida, 1988

Seventy-six years old, he says
but hung like a camel
and strong as an ox . . .

A ladies' man, a retired
small-time gangster
he says, from Detroit.

An ex-pimp is my guess
complete with gold chains
and a ridiculous bikini.

A bore, a weightlifter
a geriatric adolescent
who can walk on his hands . . .

But my mother likes him
or forgives him at least
and so do her friends—

the ladies she swims with
at the neighborhood beach.
They call him "The Hunk."

It seems he lives here—
a tent under the boardwalk
or in the palmetto somewhere.

Something to do I think
with his job—a watchman
or caretaker of some sort.

But that's not it he says.
NO! What he really does
is babysit for turtles . . .

At which point his voice
turns absolutely reverent—
as if he's speaking poetry . . .

All those little flags
sticking up out there?
Those are turtle eggs.

And on the next full moon
coincident with high tide
most of them will hatch.

That's where he comes in.
Nuncio the body builder
the lonely widow's dream

leading them to water . . .
Of course. Who else?
I can see it perfectly:

Ten thousand baby turtles
and this guy, on his hands
lurching toward the sea

where presently my mother
and her friends are sharing
a thermos of martinis . . .

How beautiful they look
bobbing around out there
in their inner tubes—

the joke on someone else
for a change, the children
on their own, at last.

5

Rush Hour

Rush hour. The busy street
of random recollection

where presently it snows.
Everyone with their lights on.

Everyone just creeping along
and not a bus in sight . . .

Outside the iron-shuttered
closed-up print shop

a boy with frozen hair
keeps looking at his watch . . .

His pointy, cardboard shoes
are soaked clear through.

His cigarettes are wet . . .
his bus tokens, everything.

And now he's late besides—
inconvenienced by the weather

as he decides to put it
while snow falls ever faster

through the purblind lights
of prehistoric, fishtailed cars

creeping toward the suburbs
where his girlfriend lives—

the one with older brothers
who maybe want to kill him.

But Oh, the powdered bristle
of her armpit! And Oh

the hard-nippled handful
of her undone breast!

What's a little inconvenience
or even frostbite next to this?

But then his bus pulls up—
an exasperated hiss of air

followed by the tired smell
of anger, wet coats, grease

a kind of tannic, sour fog
in which he falls asleep

missing his stop entirely.
And everything's so still

when at last he yawns awake
so deep in untracked snow

he can't remember for awhile
where or who he is exactly . . .

except he's on a bus somehow
a last bewildered passenger

looking down from an overpass
into a pile of wrecked cars—

some steel company junkyard
fenced and barbed with wire

that seems to him at once
indicative and unaccountable.

The end of the line, he thinks
mumbling like those old guys

full of random recollection
who wake up drunk on buses

fifteen years old again
lost in the sticks somewhere.

Catch Him!

Because a light explodes
at the busy intersection
during last night's storm

because some power lines
were just reported down

I'm walking my daughter
and some of her friends
to school. It's April . . .

one of those dream-bright
too blue mornings after days

of basement-flooding rain.
In the gusty trees, wires
hiss and spark. The trees

of course, are all berserk
and the just-bloomed tulips

tremble flat upon the ground.
Then, a blue jay suddenly
one eye plucked freshly out

fluttering on the highway
near the busy intersection . . .

Catch him! Do something!
The dancing children shout.
But it's too late for that.

We wouldn't stand a chance.
Not in this blurred traffic—

cars and buses whizzing past
as one imagines life might pass
just before we die, flickering

before the mind's stunned eye
like some corny, old-time movie

complete with subtitles: The hero
on his way to school. The hero
coming home again in tears—then

the snake pit of his homework
or gagging hours over supper . . .

years of this dreary epic
with children close by screaming:
Catch him! Do something!

before a dinner fork, let's say
stabs into his bird-sized hand.

Long Division

Inside the spiky, iron fence
of Assumption Grotto Cemetery

livelier than any daydream
obdurate as long division

a small, feathery dog
keeps racing back and forth

back and forth unceasingly
from stone to stone . . .

He seems to be chasing something—
mice, perhaps, underneath the snow.

At this distance, listening hard
his bark is barely audible

hardly anything at all . . . but
when I close my eyes

it sounds like someone crying
a muffled, headlong sobbing

I should recognize somehow . . .
Then the clock above the crucifix

jumps forward. A sudden wind
rattles the classroom windows

then lifts me by the hair . . .
Dividend! Divisor! Quotient!

our trembling nun screams out
as if I couldn't understand

plain English, couldn't hear
her ruler slapping at my book

as if I couldn't see in fact—
a child dead to the world

lost in that far graveyard
where even nuns are buried

all those good little girls
deep in their long division.

The Brave Adventure

—for Paul Friedman

I remember we had just
enlisted in the navy

my best friend and I
and so now of course

ten days from boot camp
we felt nervously agog

and sick of everything—
gas station, poolroom . . .

the whole greasy round
of the dropout unemployed.

Where were we headed anyway?
Great Lakes? San Diego?

How about Mars? But first
because we were dead center

of one last homeport winter
in Detroit, one last chance

to have some fun, we decided
we had better do something—

something we'd never forget:
like stealing a Cadillac

and driving it all night
until we ran out of gas

on frozen Lake St. Clair.
We ran out of beer too

and then the wind came up—
an honest-to-God blizzard

right out of the movies
erasing every streetlight

on fancy Lake Shore Drive.
But nevermind. My friend

knew exactly where we were.
His uncle lived out here.

In our pointy cardboard shoes
and skimpy blue suede jackets

without hats or even gloves
we'd be there in no time . . .

or on our way to Canada
and stumbling, certain death.

Meanwhile, for no good reason
beyond delinquent instinct

we walked against the wind—
all ears and frozen feet

until we accidently made it.
But afterward, for years

I'd wake up hearing ice—
those booming loud reports

behind us on the shifting ice
as if some ship were sinking . . .

the one called *Friendship* maybe
or the good bark *Brave Adventure*

stuck out there, abandoned—
crushed inexorably rib by rib.

6

The Awards Banquet

1. *What Kind of Poetry Do You Write?*

The university was thriving—
one of the best in the world
and getting better . . .

Absolutely the place to be
if you were interested at all
in superconductivity
electromagnetic imaging
or biodegradable plastics . . .

And who wasn't after all?

We were just sitting down to eat
reading each other's name tags
introducing ourselves . . . Then

by way of breaking the ice
an international genius
in high-speed computing
takes notice of the poet:

Well, so you're the poet . . .

As if I were painted blue
and wore a bone in my nose.

Next he wants to know
what kind of poetry I write—

because of course he's guessed
there must be different kinds
just as there are different kinds
of astronomy or physics . . .

When I say I write free verse
and rely for the most part
on my own experience

the whole table gets suddenly
busy with their salads.

They understand perfectly.
They wouldn't read that stuff
at gunpoint. Why should they?

They're too busy prying apart
the atom, splicing genes
planning trips to Mars
Jupiter, Alpha Centauri . . .

Besides that
no one writes in meter
and nothing rhymes anymore.

2. Squash Soup

Halfway through the squash soup
there's a disturbance . . . shouts

a loud clattering of dishes
from the chancellor's table . . .

then two campus policemen
dragging someone to the door.

The "lunatic" it turns out.
The guy in the baseball cap

who almost ruined everything—
the robotics seminar, the talk

on artificial intelligence . . .
even the poetry reading:

a hallucination almost—
there, in the front row

tight-lipped, spit whitening
the corners of his mouth

his eyes too antic-bright
his whole aspect jittery

with manic calculation . . .
until he's finally up

and shouting *Liar! Filth!*
followed by certain verses

from the Bible. God knows
what he's told the chancellor

fussing dimly with his tie . . .
A little squash soup perhaps.

Nothing really. Not blood.
Not a bullet hole at least.

And now he's even smiling.
A lunatic for Christ's sake.

What's the world coming to?
my neighbor wants to know

winking at the lovely chemist.
Tell us. You're the poet.

Meanwhile, at another table
Prometheus whispers something

to the inventor of the wheel—
then draws it on a napkin.

3. *Speech*

After dessert, it's time
for the great hall to fall silent
and face the dais.

Now the chancellor
and the vice chancellor
shall deliver their odes.

And at the sound of the ox horn
let the heroes approach
and bear off their trophies . . .

Everyone but the poet that is
who keeps falling asleep, then
snorting suddenly awake again

like one of those clever
little birds on springs
that attach to drinking glasses—

a gift, something his father
of whom he now fitfully dreams
as a matter of fact

has just brought him home
from the bar. It's winter
and there's frost on the windows.

It's after supper; a sudden
clattering of dishes, shouts . . .
and through it all the bird

bobs down and drinks over
and over from the still water
of the white kitchen table

miraculous as human speech—
a baby saying *Bird! Bird!*
there, in the black window.

Uncomfortable Procedures

—January, 1991

January, The first of six
"uncomfortable procedures"

as my periodontist puts it
putting down his scissors

with a stoic, little sigh
among the tinkling knives

still trembling on my chest.
"But let's try this," he says

loading up a fresh syringe
"let's try to get this right."

And then he disappears again
to phone his nurse, Jolene

who isn't here this morning
because her car won't start.

My doctor's clinic of course
is in the middle of nowhere

way out by Oakwood Estates
where no one even lives—

nor are there any sidewalks yet
or trees. From where I sit

waiting for my face to freeze
it's all just broken stalks

of trembling corn out there
buckets, shingles—misery

sufficient unto the day thereof
or any part that I can see

for all that blowing snow . . .
So when Jolene arrives (sorry

sorry that she's late again)
by Yellow Cab from far Rantoul

it seems a kind of miracle . . .
But it's clear she's had it—

a husband in the air force
two kids in nursery school

"and now yesterday," she says
"they go and start a goddamn war."

To which the good doctor replies:
"Can I please, if you don't mind

have a little more suction here?"
He wants to get things right.

And who knows how the null abyss
might look—the war, my mouth

all those fields out there—
once the condominiums go up

and they put a golf course in?
The thing to do is be precise—

as in precision bombing say
or surgical strikes . . . mere

uncomfortable procedures really
and over before you know it.

Late

The dog begs to go out
then whines immediately
to come back in again.

It must be twenty-five below
a fine snow sifts down
from off the roof somewhere

glittering, alive almost . . .
a blizzard of tiny fish
or phosphorescent plankton

all hypnotized no doubt
by the backdoor porchlight.
The crabapple, the lilacs

so still, so intricate
look likewise submarine—
rare black corals maybe

or arborescent lesions
deep within the brain . . .
It's after six o'clock.

And on the next block
at some impossible depth
where imagination falters

an ordinary snow shovel
scrapes its way along
through frozen drifts

of tiny skeletons, muck,
blind, anaerobic worms—
charm bracelets, shoes

the dead, literal snow
where the world escapes
its proper metaphor

and one's only child
simply misses her supper
forever and ever.

Rushing the Season

—for Emily Lynn

Late October, their pissed-off
teenaged daughter playing loud
Christmas music on the piano.

"Rushing the season?" her mother
sings from the twilight kitchen . . .

But pitched off-key, sardonic
so that her daughter understands
how things are still all right

between them—how this too
this serial, week-long argument

about clothes or hair or money
might also pass, as everything
must pass, her fourteenth fall

a fraught migration, her childhood
poignant now as that peeping bird

they thought to be a leaf at first
fluttering in the cat's mouth
next door, under the bird feeder.

And now the light out there
is otherworldly—the moon,

already high above scant trees
a smoky daylight still inhabits,
grotesque somehow, incongruous

a ship from outer space perhaps
or the diaphanous ark of extinction

drifting like a giant jellyfish
over the last rain forest—some
twin figment of her adolescence

from which, at any moment, a ladder
or a tentacle might suddenly descend.

Dreams of rescue, fells of doom
her father thinks. Who wouldn't
facing that, feel like rushing

headlong into the furious snow
of the next ice age? Someone

for some poor shepherd to discover
frozen in the wide-eyed future . . .
like that wayward, baby mastodon

found just last night on television
perfectly intact, inside a glacier.

But dead, of course. Better, then
to find some shelter—a stable
that smells like home perhaps

with pets and a decent piano
where she can wait it out—

a long, interminable pregnancy
punctuated by slamming doors, shouts
a fetal singing, joyful and triumphant.

Michael Van Walleghen

was born in 1938 in Detroit. He received his B.A. in English from Wayne State University and his M.F.A. in creative writing from the University of Iowa. He is the author of three previous books of poetry: *The Wichita Poems* (1975), *More Trouble with the Obvious* (1981), winner of the 1980 Lamont Poetry Prize of the Academy of American Poets, and *Blue Tango* (1989). Van Walleghen is professor of English at the University of Illinois, Urbana-Champaign.

PITT POETRY SERIES

Ed Ochester, General Editor

Archibald MacLeish, *The Great American Fourth of July Parade*

Peter Meinke, *Liquid Paper: New and Selected Poems*

Peter Meinke, *Night Watch on the Chesapeake*

Carol Muske, *Applause*

Carol Muske, *Wyndmere*

Leonard Nathan, *Carrying On: New & Selected Poems*

Ed Ochester and Peter Oresick, *The Pittsburgh Book of Contemporary American Poetry*

Sharon Olds, *Satan Says*

Alicia Suskin Ostriker, *Green Age*

Alicia Suskin Ostriker, *The Imaginary Lover*

Greg Pape, *Black Branches*

Greg Pape, *Storm Pattern*

Kathleen Peirce, *Mercy*

David Rivard, *Torque*

Liz Rosenberg, *Children of Paradise*

Liz Rosenberg, *The Fire Music*

Maxine Scates, *Toluca Street*

Richard Shelton, *Selected Poems, 1969–1981*

Betsy Sholl, *The Red Line*

Peggy Shumaker, *The Circle of Totems*

Peggy Shumaker, *Wings Moist from the Other World*

Jeffrey Skinner, *The Company of Heaven*

Cathy Song, *School Figures*

Leslie Ullman, *Dreams by No One's Daughter*

Constance Urdang, *Alternative Lives*

Constance Urdang, *Only the World*

Michael Van Walleghen, *Tall Birds Stalking*

Ronald Wallace, *The Makings of Happiness*

Ronald Wallace, *People and Dog in the Sun*

Belle Waring, *Refuge*

Michael S. Weaver, *My Father's Geography*

Robley Wilson, *Kingdoms of the Ordinary*

Robley Wilson, *A Pleasure Tree*

David Wojahn, *Glassworks*

David Wojahn, *Late Empire*

David Wojahn, *Mystery Train*

Paul Zimmer, *Family Reunion: Selected and New Poems*